Birds of Africa

Kenya and Tanzania

Jane Moorman

Photographer's Comments

Seeing the animals in the wild is always a thrill, whether they are buffalo in Yellowstone National Park, or elephants in Africa.

While creating a book of bird photographs I had taken on various day trips and vacations, I realized I wanted to take photos of the wild animals in Africa.

I have had a special place in my heart for giraffes since feeding them at the Cheyenne Mountain Zoo in Colorado Springs, Colorado. I wanted to see this majestic animal in the wild.

During the third year of my retirement, I headed to Africa for an 18-day tour of national wildlife reserves in Kenya and Tanzania. Using a Sony RX10iv camera with its built-in 24-600 zoom lens, I took 4,000 photos.

I have never been much of a birdwatcher, but fortunately, the guide of our Kenya African Safari, knows the birds when he sees them at a distance. Sometimes, it took looking through the binoculars to help identify them, but most of the time, Samuel M. Wawer did it on the move while driving the safari tour truck on bumpy, dirt roads.

I captured photos of 42 different birds.

Enjoy!

Jane Moorman, photographer

Amazing Birdwatching

Photographing birds is tricky. First, you need to see the birds in their natural habitat; then, you need to get it in-focus before it takes flight.

Fortunately, the guide of our Kenya African Safari, knew the birds when he sees them at a distance. Sometimes, it took looking through the binoculars to help identify them, but most of the time, Samuel M. Wawer did it on the move while driving the safari tour truck on bumpy, dirt roads.

I would not have as many of these photos if it had not been for him.

East Africa's birdlife is remarkable, and few people can fail to be impressed by the large variety of colorful birds.

Some 1,400 or more species have been recorded in East Africa, which represents approximately 15 percent of the world's total.

I have organized this book by the type of species, such as birds of prey, water waders, web feet, etc.

The biggest thrill for me as a photographer is when I catch a bird in flight with their wings extended. To get a shot that is in-focus where the detail of the feathers is visible is quite an accomplishment. None of these photos were taken from a blind, where I sat for hours waiting. They were taken in a moment's notice, when Sam pointed them out to us.

Jane Moorman

Birds of Prey

African Fish Eagle

Length: Male 25 inches, female 28 inches (63, 73 cm)
Feeds on fish, catches by swooping down and snatching them from the water.

African Crowned Eagle

Length: 31 to 39 inches (80-99 cm)

Very large eagle, it is the fifth longest extant eagle in the world. Its crown is dark to rufous-brown with a permanent, oft-raised black-tipped double crest. The wing primaries (features) are white at the base, broadly tipped with black and crossed by two black bars. The adult crowned eagle has eyes that can range from yellow to almost white.

The crowned eagle is found only on the continent of Africa.

Long-crested Eagle

Length: 20-24 inches (52-58 cm)

Small eagle with a distinctive, long, loose crest. The body is dark brownish black, which contrasts with the white feathered legs. Eyes are yellow.

African Harrier Hawk

Length: 23-26 inches (60-66 cm) Distinctive long-legged, long-tailed grey hawk. The head is small and has bare yellow skin on the face. In flight, the broad, grey wings, with contrasting black primaries and secondaries, and the long, black tail with a white band, distinctive.

Long-legged Waders
Sandpiper-like Birds
Duck-like Birds

Goliath Heron

Length: 55-59 inches (140-152 cm) The world's largest heron. Its size, bushy crest on the top of the crown and large, heavy bill are distinctive. The call is a distinctive 'karrrk.'

Greater Flamingo

Length: 50-55 inches (127-142 cm)

Much larger and less common than Lesser Flamingo. Feeds by filtering small invertebrates from the bottom mud in shallow waters. You can tell the difference in the Greater and Lesser flemingos by how deep they put their bill in the water, the Greater is totally submerges, while the Lesser skim the top.

Lesser Flamingo

Length: 32– 35 inches (81-90 cm)

A surface feeder, filtering blue-green algae from the top few inches of the water.

Juvenile have gray plumage.

Grey Crowned Crane

Length: 49 inches (102 cm) Has a conspicuous, large, golden-yellow crown, a bright, white patch on the cheeks, a black forehead and small red wattles. Upperparts are slate-grey, the underparts paler and the wing is blackish with distinctive white-tinged chestnut patch

Grey Heron

Length: 35-39 inches (90-100 cm)

A distinctive grey neck with a line of black streaks down the front. The white forehead and crown contrast strongly with a black line that runs from behind the eyes and ends in a wispy crest.

Glossy Ibis

Length: 19-26 inches (48-66 cm)

Plumage appears dark, almost blackish, at a distance or in poor light. At close range, much of the body is maroon, with a wing covert showing metallic green, bronze, and violet tones.

Yellow-billed Egret

Length: 24-27 inches (61-69 cm)

Considerably small than the Great White Egret. Shorter necked with a stumpy yellow bill. The eyes are yellow with a black line extending from the gape ends immediately below the eyes.

African Spoonbill

Length: 36 inches (91 cm) Has an unmistakable flattened, spoon-shaped bill.

Giant Kingfisher

Length: 16-18 inches (42-46 cm)

Large shaggy crest, a large black bill, and fine white spots on black upperparts. The male has a chestnut breast band and white underparts with dark flank barring. Feeds on crabs, fish and frogs, caught by diving from a perch.

Pied Kingfisher

Length: 9 inches (25 cm)

A highly social, black-and-white kingfisher with a crested head and a long, black bill. The male has two black bands across the white chest, while the female has one incomplete band. Commonly hunts for fish by hovering before diving, beak-first into water.

Long-toed Lapwing

Length: 12 inches (31 cm)

One of 13 species of ground-nesting lapwings found in Africa. It is a brown, black and white lapwing

with long red legs, long toes and

Blacksmith Plover (Lapwing)

Length: 11 1/2 inchs (30 cm)

A large, conspicuous, black-and-white plover with deep-red eyes (difficult to see), a black bill and black legs. Earned its name when alarmed, its call is a very distinctive, metallic 'tink tink' like a blacksmith hammering metal.

African Jacana

Length: 9-11 inches (23-28 cm)

Chestnut-colored bird with long legs and long toes. The head has a black crown and hindneck, a white face and a white foreneck with a golden-yellow band at the base. The bill and frontal shield are blue.

The females are polyandrous, mate with several males, and only the males incubate the

Great White Pelican

Length: 55-71 inches (140-180 cm)

Feeds on freshwater fish. Bill is huge, blue-pink with a yellow pouch.

White-breasted Cormorant

Length: 31-39 inches (80-100 cm)

Noticeable hook-tipped bill. White cheeks, throat and upper breast and often a distinctive white patch on the side of the rump.

Pied Avocet

Length: 16.5-17.75 inches (41-45 cm)

A striking white wader with bold black markings. Adults have white plumage except for a black cap and black patches in the wings and on the back. They have long, upturned bills and long, bluish legs.

Red-billed Teal

Length: 16-18 inches (43-48 cm) Distinguished by red bill and dark cap, which contrasts with its pale cheeks.

Cape teal

Chicks sleeping in a circle around the parent ducks. Adult length: 17-19 inches (44-48 cm).

Egyptian Goose

Length: 24 to 28 inches (63-67 cm)

Has a conspicuous rufous-colored patch around the eyes.

Knob-billed Duck

Length: 22-30 inches (56-76 cm)

White head freckled with dark spots and a pure white neck and underparts. The upperparts are glossy blue-black with bluish and greenish iridescence especially prominent on the lower wing feathers. Flanks are usually light gray. Male has a large black knob on the bill.

White-faced Whistling Duck

Lenth: 16-18 inches (43-48 cm) The ducks name reflects its clear, whistling, three-note call.

Red-knobbed Coot

Length: 16 inches (41 cm)

A dark grey water bird with a distinctive white forehead and white bill. The eyes are deep red and there are two red knobs above the forehead, which are often visible only during breeding. Dives for food but also feeds along the shoreline.

Ground Birds

Ostrich

Length: 8 feet (2-2.5 meters)

Kori Bustard

Length: 5 feet tall. Male kori bustards range in weight from 24-42 pounds, and females are roughly half the size of the male. It is hard to believe from this photo that this bird is the largest flying bird native to Africa. They spend most of their time on the ground, with up to 70 percent of their time being on foot. When alarmed it will first run and, if pushed further, will take to the air with much effort. It usually flies low and lands again within sight.

Yellow-necked Spurfowl

Length: 13-16 inches (34-43 cm)

Distinctive-looking spurfowl with a bright yellow throat and bare, red skin around the eyes.

Helmeted Guineafowl

Length: 22-25 inches (58-64 cm) Spends most of the time on the ground, but roosts in trees.

Perching Birds

Lilac-breasted Roller

Length 16 inches (41 cm)

A striking, common bird with a bright lilac throat and breast, deep-blue underparts and distinctive, elongated outer tail feathers. The back is olive-chestnut and the wings have dark blue converts.

Purple Roller

Length: 14-16 inches (35-40 cm)

From a distance it appears a dull brownish bird with a white stripe over the eye, a patch of white on the nape and a dark tail.

Speckled Mousebird

Length: 13 inches (33 cm)

Brown bird with a very long tail and distinctive head crest. The body feathers are edged with white, imparting a speckled appearance. The face is black, with white cheek patches, the bill is black above and pinkish below. The legs are red.

Greater Blue-eared Starling

Length: 9 inches (23 cm)

The upperparts are bluer, darkening on the belly. Eyes are striking orange-yellow, contrasting with the dark, blackish ear coverts.

Common Bulbul

Length: 7 inches (18 cm)

It has a distinctive yellow undertail coverts. Feathers on the nape often raises, giving the head a crested appearance.

The distinctive call, a rapid 'towee-too tweeoo' is often translated as 'Come back to Calcutta."

Superb Starling

Length: 7 inches (18 cm)

Eastern Africa's best-known starling, with iridescent, blue-green upperparts and black spots on the wings. The head is blackish and the eyes are pale yellow. The belly is rich orange-chestnut, separated from the throat by a narrow white line.

Feeds on the ground, eating mainly insects, but also occasionally fruit, Acacia flowers and seeds.

Very prevalent at parking lots and picnic areas.

Speke's Weaver

Length: 6 inches (15 cm)

Males have yellow forehead, crown and nape. The back is yellow, with distinctive black marking. Sides of face, chin, throat and bill are black. Eyes are

Baglafecht Weaver

Length: 6 inches (15 cm) The male in Kenya has a black nape, back, tail and eye coverts. Females have a black crown and face.

Eastern Double-collared Sunbird

Length: 4 inches (10 cm) The curved bill is used to sip nectar from flowers.

Scavengers

Marabou Stork

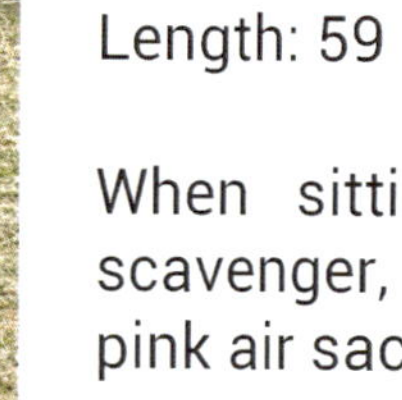

Length: 59 inches (152 cm)

When sitting, legs hinge forwards, compared to humans. A scavenger, but also feeds on rodents and insects. An extendable pink air sac hangs down from the throat.

Lappet-faced Vulture

Length: 37-45 inches (95-115 cm) with a wingspan of 8.2-9.5 feet (2.5-2.9 m).

The combination of the dull red or pink head with fleshy folds on the side of it are distinctive of this species.

White-backed Vulture

Length: 35-38.5inches (89-98 cm) A large, uniformly brown vulture has a long almost-bare neck with a pale ruff at its base. The white back and rump are seen only in flight. Inmature distinquished from mature Rappiell's Vulture by its darker appearance and shorter bill.

Ruppell's Griffon Vulture

Length: 37-42 inches (95-107 cm) Distinguished by a creamy-white edging in the body and wing feathers, which gives it's a scaly appearance. Head and almost-bare neck are grey with sparse, whitish down. The bill horn-colored, tinged pink.

About the Photographer

Jane Moorman describes herself as an adventurer who loves to drive the backroads to see what there is to see.

During her 30-year journalism career, Jane honed her photographic skills as a photo journalist including covering high school sporting events.

A friend once said, "I wish I could see the world as Jane sees it. Finding the beauty in things that most of us don't take time to see."

Upon retiring in 2021, Jane decided there is a lot of her native country she had not visited, including each state's capitol, so she began her journey of exploring the USA.

During 2023, Jane visited two places on her bucket list — Kenya for an African Safari and Switzerland to see the Alps.

She currently lives in Albuquerque, New Mexico, but says her real home is on the road.

When she is not on the road, she is home building photo books of what she has seen.

She currently has published books of the Great Lake Lighthouses and United States state capitols, as well as other interesting things she has discovered during her travels.

Other books in the works includes Switzerland by train, visiting three mountains by cog trains; Budapest; cathedrals of Europe; and United States east and west coast light houses.

Her books are available on Amazon.com and other digital book platforms.

Source

Information regarding the length and weight of the animals if from "Wildlife of East Africa: A photographic Guide," by Dave Richards. Published by Struik Nature, Random House Struik Ltd.

www.ingramcontent.com/pod-product-compliance
Ingram Content Group UK Ltd.
Pitfield, Milton Keynes, MK11 3LW, UK
UKRC032027290726
14090UKWH00008B/484

* 9 7 9 8 3 3 0 5 7 1 3 5 2 *